The Virtual Tablet of Irma Tre

The Virtual Tablet of Irma Tre

by Marie Lecrivain

Edgar & Lenore's Publishing House
Los Angeles 2014

Published by
Edgar & Lenore's Publishing House

Copyright © 2014

Published in the United States of America

www.edgarallanpoet.com

Cover Art by Kevin Abblett
Interior photos by Marie Lecrivain
Cover design by Apryl Skies

Library of Congress Cataloging-in-Publication Data
Marie Lecrivain

The Virtual Tablet of Irma Tre
by Marie Lecrivain – First Edition

ISBN-13: 978-0985471545
ISBN-10: 0985471549
(Edgar & Lenore's Publishing House)
Library of Congress Control Number: 2014932085

Manufactured in the United States of America
First Edition

Table of Contents

Foreword viii

Antimony 13
Bain-Marie 15
Cinnabar 17
Distillation 19
Egg 21
Fixation 23
Geber 25
Hemaphrodite 27
Iron 29
Jung 31
King 33
Liquor Hepatis 35
Mercury 37
Natron 39
Oroboros 41
Pulvis Solaris 43
Quintessence 45
Retort 47
Stone 49
Trituration 51
Uroboros 53
Vitriol 55
Wine 57
Xanthosis/Yellow Phase 59
Zodiac 60

Biography 62
Artist Biography\Editor Biography 63
Acknowledgements 64

The Universe is an ongoing experiment in alchemy. Everything I do is alchemy, including writing poetry. This little book is the result of six years spent living the life of a ceremonial magician in an hermetic fraternal order where I study and experience alchemy on a microcosmic/macrocosmic level. The initial inspiration for the poems comes from the *Alchemy Electronic Dictionary* (http://www.alchemylab.com/dictionary.htm).
The title is an homage to *The Emerald Tablet of Hermes Trismegistus*.

Alchemy is evolution. To deny that fact would to deny my whole existence, and that is something I am – gladly – no longer able to do. - *M.L. aka Sr. Barbelo*

This little book is dedicated with respect and affection to: Charles Claymore, J Sabrina McGuire, Craig Berry, Sigrid Bishop, Deborah Warner, Jon Cunningham, Apryl Skies, Lon and Constance Duquette, Dave and Lynne Scriven, Leanne Brooks, Michelle Angelini, Suzanne Torchia, Rafael Aguilar, Lita-Luise Chappell and Vere Chappell, Kevin Abblett, Sondra Scott, Mike and Kathy Rogers, Cindy Weinstein, Brenda Petrakos, Angel Uriel Perales, Thoth, Seshat, Santa Muerte, and my biological family.

Foreword

The Virtual Tablet of Irma Tre explores the correlation between poetry and alchemy through a series of alphabetized poetic vignettes, and evocative photography.

Additionally, the poems of this collective speak directly to the reader's past, present, and future selves. Exploring the idea of reincarnation, Lecrivain expresses the importance of evolving the Self for a greater good through catharsis and cognizance.

> *"There's no malice*
> *in the transmission of knowledge.*
> *It's an inborn impulse,*
> *embedded in the back wall*
> *of the left ventricle*
> *that drags all incarnations*
> *to the present."* – Geber

While this tome is by no means a "self-help manual" and, in no way forcefully didactic, it is, in some light, much like a poetical guidebook for transforming one's higher Self into spiritual gold.

Lecrivain presents the philosophy of alchemy in a transcendental sense to create a bridge of understanding that enlightens the reader. Through this labyrinth of artistic ablution the reader is cleansed of negativity and moves toward a higher consciousness, in turn the subconscious is also purified.

This is not the extent of what the author accomplishes in *The Virtual Tablet*, Lecrivain has employed elementals to represent this philosophy through clever metaphor, hard-won truths, humor and sword-wielding wit.

"Fortified with intent, it's the weapon of your soul. Use it carefully..." – Iron

And in "Ouroboros" and the opposing "Uruboros", Lecrivain challenges convention using satire to not only amuse, but reflect modern day society in a light-hearted yet tangible and palpable execution.

The Virtual Tablet of Irma Tre ceases to preach this philosophy, but rather inspires the reader to heal through strength of character, strong constitution and creativity, thus turning negativity into something of value and virtue, i.e. growth.

> *"Once you behold all*
> *of creation in an orange halo,*
> *you've attained your goal."*- Pulvis Solaris

In closing, many of the best writers, authors, and artists are truly sages, unconsciously, instinctually teachers in the humblest form. A prime example of this is the following passage:

> *"...a pebble skipped across*
> *the streams of time,*
> *this is you - from life to life -*
> *at your quintessential best."* - Stone

Simply through the selfless and intriguing act of creating art from experience and wisdom these artists are able to educate, often unbeknownst to both the mentor and apprentice. What Lecrivain has achieved here is pure illumination.

~Apryl Skies

If thou but settest foot on this path, thou shalt see it everywhere. - Hermes Trismegistus

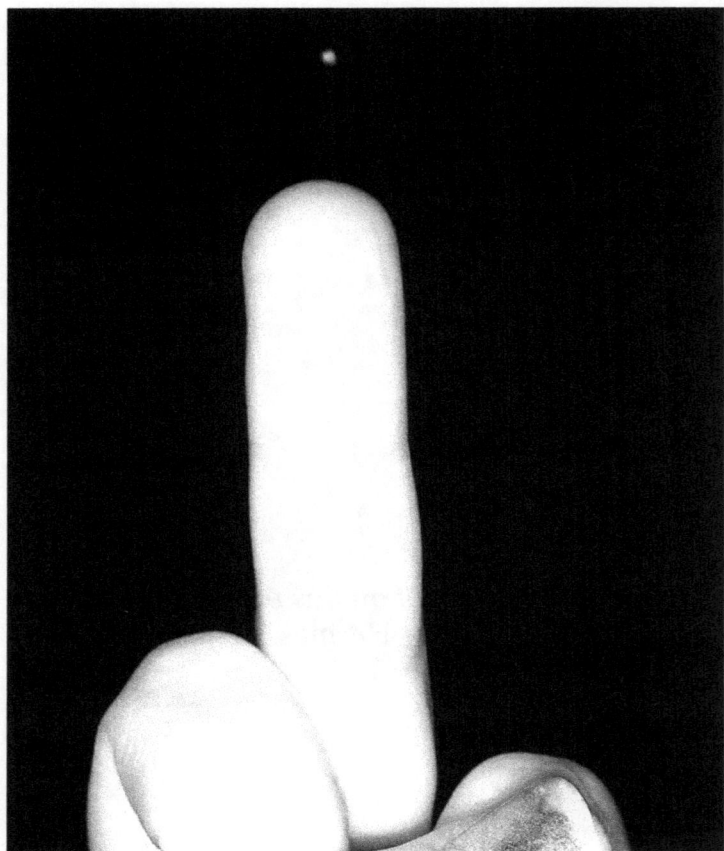

Antimony

Part of herself on the periphery is a wolf-woman who awakens at 3 am, fierce and sweating from dreams of rending apart the poisoned flesh of her enemies. She follows the retreating image of her dark, desperate face in the glowing disk of the Western Moon, already on a downward trajectory to escape her question: *Why did you summon me?* With no answers, she gifts the heavens a hairy middle-fingered salute, and with one last howl, encloses herself in a slumbering cage of meat and bone. She will awaken at dawn, confused by the musky scent of anima imprinted on the tangle of rent sheets.

Bain-marie

In Maria P's soul kitchen, it sits on the back of the stove next to the teapot, to be employed on the following occasions: holidays and cross-quarters, weddings and funerals, and emergencies like when the heart is broken. This is the time to put yourself in the capable hands of Madame Maria P. She will make you tea and read you stories from the *Book of Life,* while your heart, enclosed in copper and stainless steel, simmers in aqua vitae. When your heart is healed, it will be carefully placed and sewn back into your chest with the admonition: *When you join the male with the female, you'll find nothing but trouble.*

Cinnabar

You and I smash
against the walls
of our souls. We work
to create openings
large enough to escape
the other's ennui.

Disappointment bleeds
into the dusty ground.
Exhausted and empty,
we carefully place
curious fingers into the cracks
of our fissured selves,
with tender appreciation
for new dimensions.

Distillation

It's time to give up. The bony finger beckons to cast aside flesh. It doesn't matter how old or young you are - the invitation comes once - and *only* once.

She takes you by the hand; that which remains glows albic in the astral light. This is the time to focus on what, where, and who you will become on your next turn of the wheel, the centrifuge of incarnation that separates the karmic detritus of your past and future selves.

In the moment between a last breath and the first wail, this intent is your greatest asset.

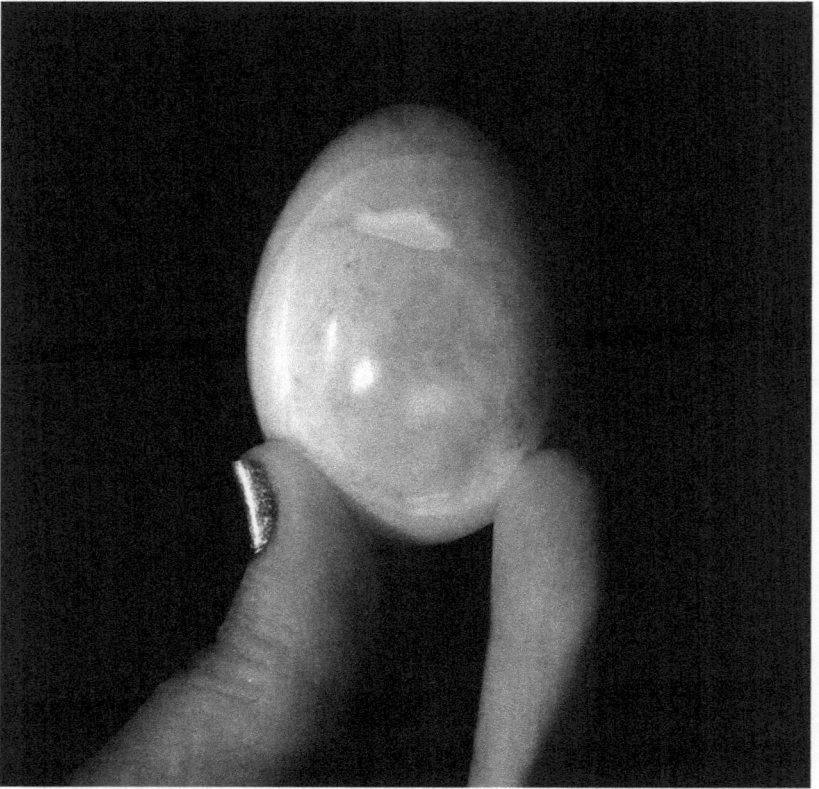

Egg

Your mind inside the bone cage,
atop the meat structure,
marinates for years.

The putrefaction starts
in the 5/6th decades.
As time runs backwards,
all your achievements
and mental constructs
are stripped away.
The unmasked myelin
scream a continuous
subsonic whine.
This farce can only end
in one of three ways;
an ischemic benediction,
a hammer to the forehead, or
a fall off the wall.

Fixation

... with apologies to Swinburne...

You've come to the right place.

The twins on either side of you
wear masks over mouthless faces.
You can see their eyes
tell the same story;
kindness kills.

They're professionals.
They can fix anything,
including the chronic problem
of change and causation
that plagues your cushy life.

Don't worry about the twins
as they mentally hem and haw
over where to drill. Soon,
you'll be asleep,
and when you awake
you'll always be a *sleep.*

Geber

With Promethean intent
he'll find his way to you.

He's the pharmacist
who regales you
with tales of what happens
to the unwary who mix
SSRIs with chardonnay.

He's the mismatched JPL nerd
who lives to fulminate
over the demise of Jack Parsons
at cocktail parties.

There's no malice
in the transmission of knowledge.
It's an inborn impulse,
embedded in the back wall
of the left ventricle
that drags all incarnations
to the present.
It's the maxim
that remains unproven,
since science as karma
is largely misunderstood.
Be patient, and kind.
He's keeps trying
and *trying*
and trying
until he gets it right.

Hermaphrodite

Those little voices in your head are the quicksilver imp seated on your left shoulder who whispers naughty thoughts at the speed of light and the righteous mouse on the opposite side who digs his claws into your shoulder with exquisite disapproval.

In the moment you're faced with a pivotal choice, these two disparates embrace and dissolve into the crannies of your cerebellum. You can move forward into the singularity of silence.

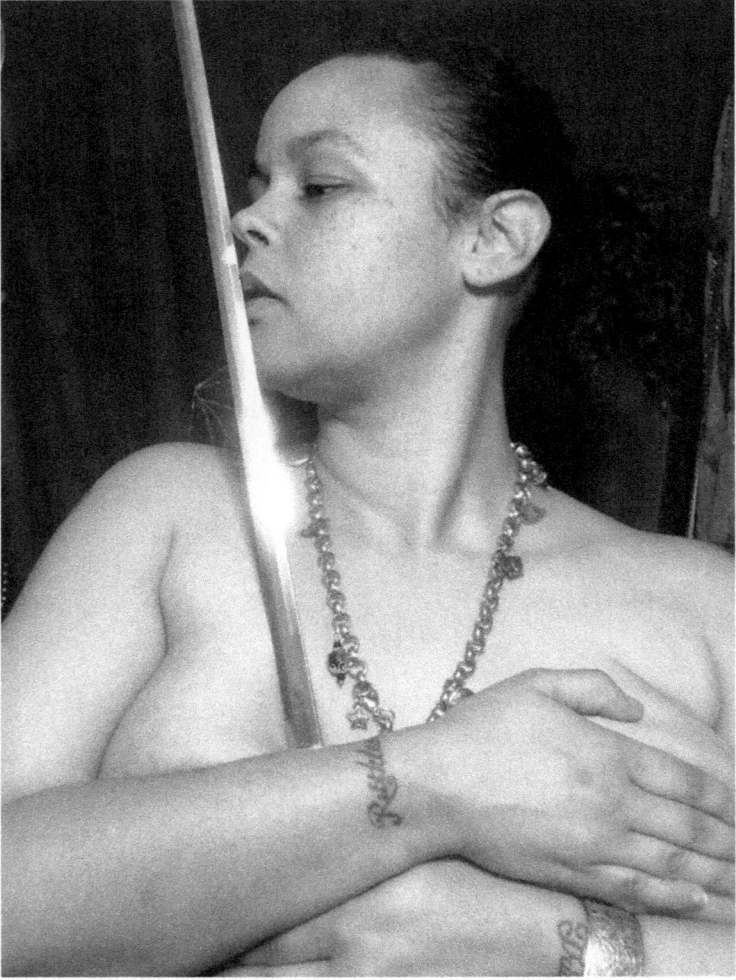

Iron

In the blood of the spine, there's a sword that never breaks, whose blade never

rusts. Fortified with intent, it's the weapon of your soul. Use it carefully, with no

objections and never in anger. If you follow these instructions to the letter, then

no one dares cross you in times of war or peace - unless you're a fool.

Jung

there once was a man named Carl
whose dreams began to unsnarl
he discovered the key
to subconscious alchemy
beneath his emotional marl

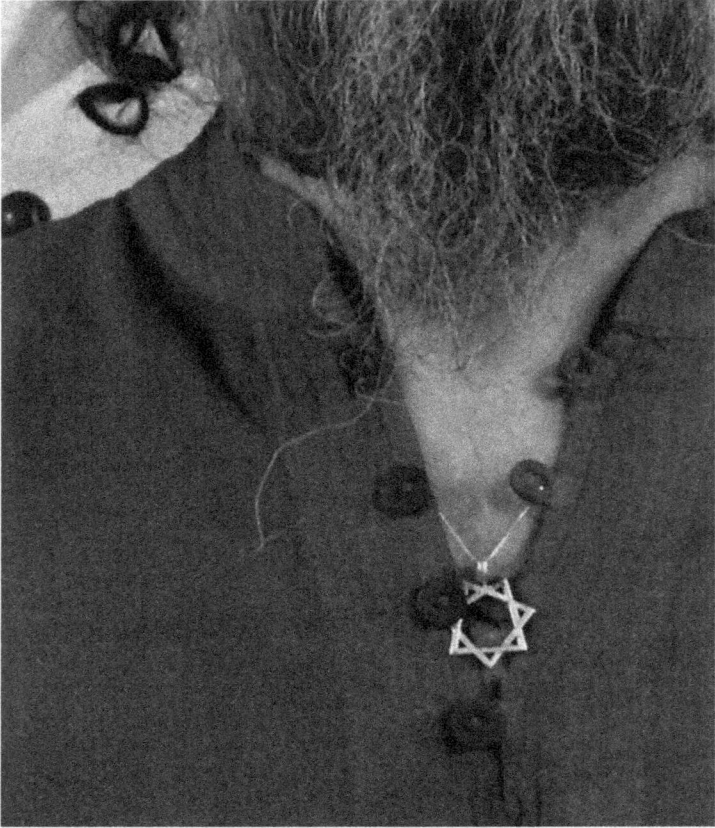

King

A man among men,
he starts off like every other.
Ejected naked from the womb,
he looks for a good time,
sustenance, all of it -
the inheritance of his destiny:
the samite boxers;
Savile Row single-breasted red suit;
gold fleur de lis pinky ring,
and finally, the crown atop
the rooster-shaped pompadour.

His date, the Queen,
manifests from beyond the pale:
a vision in virginal blue negligee;
white slender limbs open to receive,
and long red hair tumbles down her back.
His staff is at the ready.
Let us turn down the lights
and let the conjuncture commence.

Liquor Hepatis

Yes. Your shit stinks.
So does mine. I'm not talking
about the excretory end
after an evening at McDonald's.
I speak to the septic wounds
deep within ourselves,
ignored and neglected
in the press of everyday concerns.
There is a way
to turn loss into profit.
Keep a peripheral eye
on the inner fermentation.
You begin to see
at the soul's atomic level,
the small and vast miracle of change
that happens without and within.
To the uninitiated
this reeks of masochism,
but to those of us
who ripen with wisdom,
we learn how to mark the time,
to be ready for that day
when we expose the wound
to the unblemished fire of truth,
and we're rewarded with
with a sweet-smelling
and unforgettable scar.

Mercury

We joke about you
in winged retrograde
and wearing assless chaps,
your quicksilver nature
that dissolves or solidifies
a mortal's destiny
in an instant.

Why gambol about
like a fly in the face
of an oncoming train?
Mercury, there are
more than a few of us
who understand
you're the arbiter
of the sacred
and the profane,
and in the grand scheme
our lives last as long
as the turn of a dime.

We yearn to capture
more than a fleeting glance
of your winsome face,
to us, a blessing and
a moment of grace.

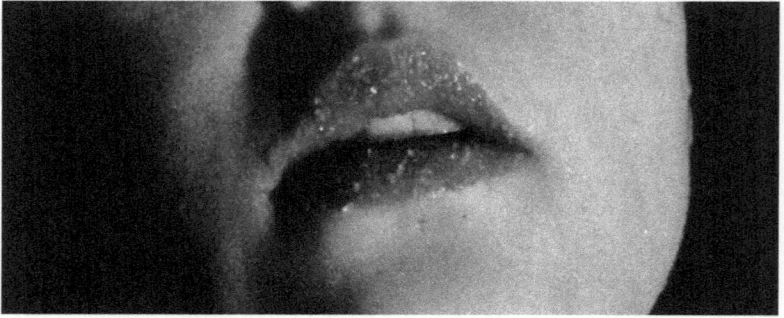

Natron

She's a vision of the color spectrum;
albic skin, black hair, pink lips,
gray eyes to die for - and, maybe so.

Beware of where and when you meet her -
basement bars or by the seaside
on a moonlit night. She's quiet
and quixotic like the tides
that run her blood. One moment
she's poised to run, the next,
she's melting in your arms
with an acidic and tender love.
It's too late. You're a *goner*...
And you'll remember nothing
as you lift your aching head
to dawn's early light.
You'll wonder how she escaped,
the only mark of her existence
a gritty crescent of salty crystals
embedded to your lips.

Ouroboros

"Hello. It's nice to meet you. My name is Mrs. Harris. I'm the Director of Human Resources for Oblivio Industries. Would you like something to drink? Oh, okay. Let's see. Yes, I have your CV right here. It says under "Work History," that you've had one job - for an aeon. That's a *long* time. Well, that's all right. We like a show of loyalty, and there's advantages for an employee who'll stick with the company. It also says under "Special Skills," that you can maintain a singular focus, you really love to sink your teeth into a project, and that you'll grab opportunities by the tail. I see you mean that literally. Hmmm. Would you say that you're people-oriented? What's that? I'm sorry, I didn't quite catch what you said. Oh! You don't like to talk with your mouth full. Well, Mr. O, I think we have all we need. I'll give you a call and let you know either way what our final decision will be. Thank you for coming in. It was a pleasure to meet you and have a good afternoon."

Pulvis Solaris

There are various ways to obtain
the most treasured of substances.
Stand outside for seven nights
under the auspices of Saturn and
Mercury. Count in breaths of seven
on the way to *le petite mort*.
Scale the seven hills of Rome
during the summer solstice.

Once you behold all
of creation in an orange halo,
you've attained your goal.

Quintessence

The secret is to reach out to both sides
of the spectrum and combine them into
a moment of grace. Go and take The Bride's
alabaster hand. She's waiting for you
to return her to the Sun, the one whose
light radiates at midnight. Here He is,
hand held out to you in welcome. Don't lose
this moment. Take the proffered palm. His
warmth is intense but true. The connection
established, your voices ascend in song,
a sweet trio attuned to the vibration
of the Cosmos. There's no need to prolong
the ecstasy from above or below;
from this perfect union will new life flow.

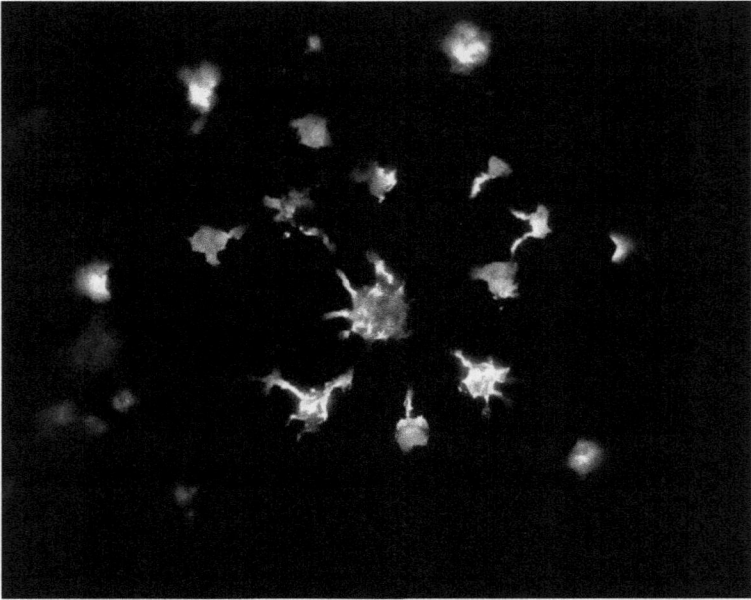

Retort

We are all too familiar with the process -
the little wounds, the cutting and careless remarks
that gather down in the lowest part of the gut
where they ferment for years.
The pain generates
a constant parting
of oft-bitten lips into
an approximation of a smile.

Soon, you are Vesuvius,
belching a constant stream of smoke and ash
that the denizens you hold near and dear
will ignore. It'll be *after* the upward current
of vomitous rage, as your eyes glow
with righteous anger, that the words
will come, the rational explanation
of *why*, but then, it will be too late.

Look, the plain is empty.
You annihilated that which
will no longer harm you.
Enjoy the silence.

Stone

Everything you've ever
worked for comes down
to the most quotidian of objects.
Look closer. There is nothing
without the earth. No alchemy,
astronomy, architecture,
art, the list goes on...
There is no beginning
without proper building material,
no foundation
from which we can evolve.
Whether it be a boulder
on which to build our kingdom
or a pebble skipped across
the streams of time,
this is you - from life to life -
at your quintessential best.
Even the cobblestones
have a great destiny.

Trituration

Most aspirants fail at this stage.
First came the violence of birth,
the dichotomous joy of life,
and finally, the winnowing of death.
You'd think we'd be done. But, no,
we all end up in the same place,
in the palm of the Universe
ready to be crushed
and tossed back
among the stars.
What is the secret to be willing,
to welcome the walls as they close in
to pulverize what little remains?
Remember: All of this has happened before,
and will again. It won't lessen the pain,
but it will put a smile on your face.

Uruboros

Dear Mr. U,

Thank you for your interest in our corporation, but the position has been filled. We'll keep your application on file for future employment opportunities as they become available.

Very truly yours,
Mrs. Harris
Director, Human Resources
Oblivio Industries, LLC

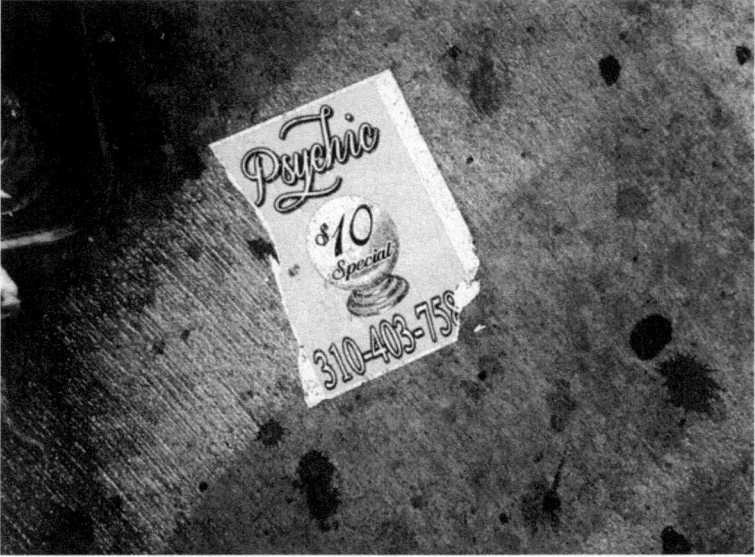

Vitriol

We never thank the ones who murder us,
whose words strike at the heart of who we are
and leave behind a tiny acidic barb
that wears away our memories of who they were,
as well as our illusions who we wished them to be.

We never appreciate the death of love,
the dull and dreary days we slog through,
the sleepless nights we waste
weeping into their pillow.
In the throes of grief,
we're unable to see
the refinement as it happens
in real time, until one day
we awaken, tearless
and excited, for the first time
in years. We rush to the mirror
and find a new face there to greet us.
Congratulations. Now, you understand.

Wine

(ghazal)

There is truth in whiskey as well as wine.
The years ripen our hearts like a fine wine.

We toast best-laid plans met with success.
We wash away failure with each sip of wine.

We search for answers inside the glass.
Finding none, we drown our sorrows in wine.

The deepest and most profound thoughts
ferment inside us like a cask of wine.

Between the first breath and the last exhale,
we're sure to imbibe a steady flow of wine.

We're all grapes on the cosmic vine.
There's truth in whiskey as well as wine.

Xanthosis/Yellow Phase

Intellectual/Intuitive
Rational/Mutable
Fearful/Courageous
Stubborn/Acquiescent
Logic/Passion
Peace/War
Word/Will
Compromise
Conjunction
Inspiration
Poet--

Zodiac

What the sleepers don't know is this:

Thomas was a Virgo - literally!

Peter, not Jesus, was a Capricorn
who couldn't see the pebble for the mountain.
John was a Libra in the best and worst sense
of the word (it ultimately saved his ass).

Both Jameses were born a day apart.
A Cancer and a Leo, respectively, they worked
stealthily and well together.

Andrew was a Pisces who fished for answers
in the deep well of the unconscious.

Philip was an Aquarian; always last to the party
and first in the esoteric know.

Nathaniel was a Taurus;
the less said of him the better.
Matthew's Scorpion nature allowed him
to transcend the literati.

Simon, the Gemini Zealot, allowed
the dichotomy within to still
the dagger in his hand.

Jude, a typical Aries, found his way
into the heart of the matter.

And Judas the Sag pointed the way.

Of The Magdalen and The Christos,
we can only say this:

The *hieros gamos* was attended and witnessed
by twelve guests, and though none of them
checked the wedding registry,
there was enough wine for everyone
to participate in the wedding toast.

ABOUT THE AUTHOR

Marie Lecrivain is the executive editor and publisher of *poeticdiversity: the litzine of Los Angeles*, a Pushcart Prize nominee, photographer, and is a writer in residence at her apartment.

Her prose and poetry have appeared in a number of journals and anthologies, including: *Edgar Allan Poet Journal, Haibun Today, The Los Angeles Review, The Poetry Salzburg Review, San Gabriel Valley Poetry Quarterly, Spillway, Tree Killer Ink, A New Ulster*, and others.

Marie's chapbook of poetry, *Love Poems... Yes... REALLY... Love Poems*, (copyright 2013 Sybaritic Press), is available through Amazon.com. She is also the editor of several anthologies, including *Near Kin: Words and Art inspired by O.E. Butler* (© 2014 Sybaritic Press).

Her avocations include alchemy; alternate modes of transportation; her cats Puff, and Guinness; expensive handbags; H.P. Lovecraft; knitting; Libers XV and LXV, Vincent Price, steampunk accessories, and the letter "S."

ABOUT THE ARTIST

Kevin Abblett is an artist and aspiring writer living in Scottsdale, Az. He spends his time primarily in studies and reflection, and in enjoying the life he and his amazing lady friend are building for themselves. He is passionately spiritual and seeks to reveal something of his esoteric experience through his numerous creations. He can be found through his blog: Gnosticprints.wordpress.com

ABOUT THE EDITOR

(This biography has been included by the gracious insistence of the author.)

Apryl Skies is a Los Angeles, award-winning poet and filmmaker. As founder of Edgar & Lenore's Publishing House, a small press publisher, she expresses her creativity and emotion with a lyrical musicality and a quiet intensity. Author of several books, her writing has gained acclaim both locally and internationally.

Publication Credits

"Antimony," "Hermaphrodite," and "Pulvis Solaris" appeared in *Dual Coast Magazine* (Vol 1, 2014)

"Cinnabar" appeared in the anthology, *The Art of Being Human, Vol. 9: The Best Poetry of 2013* (edited by Danila Voicu and Brian Wrixon, copyright 2014 Blurb Publishing)

"Mercury," appeared in *A New Ulster* (Issue #16, Jan 2014)

"Virtriol" appeared in *vox poetica* (Feb. 23, 2014)

"Wine," and "Egg" appeared in *Cultural Weekly* (week of Jan 8, 2014, www.culturalweekly.com)

"Stone" appeared/will appear in *Orbis 166* (Spring 2014), and *Paper Nautilus* (Autumn 2014).

"Retort" appeared in *Maitenant #8*, Three Rooms Press, (May 2014)

www.ingramcontent.com/pod-product-compliance
Lightning Source LLC
LaVergne TN
LVHW041236080426
835508LV00011B/1244